MAKING A BULLY-FREE
WORLD

Text by Pamela Hall
Illustrations by Bob Ostrom

magic
wagon

Content Consultant
Finessa Ferrell, Director,
National Center for School Engagement

visit us at www.abdopublishing.com

Published by Magic Wagon, a division of the ABDO Group, PO Box 398166, Minneapolis, MN 55439. Copyright © 2013 by Abdo Consulting Group, Inc. International copyrights reserved in all countries. All rights reserved. No part of this book may be reproduced in any form without written permission from the publisher.

Looking Glass Library™ is a trademark and logo of Magic Wagon.

Printed in the United States of America, North Mankato, Minnesota.
032012
092012

THIS BOOK CONTAINS AT LEAST 10% RECYCLED MATERIALS.

Text by Pamela Hall
Illustrations by Bob Ostrom
Edited by Holly Saari
Series design and cover production by Craig Hinton
Interior production by Kelsey Oseid

Library of Congress Cataloging-in-Publication Data

Hall, Pamela, 1961-
  Making a bully-free world / by Pamela Hall ; illustrated by Bob Ostrom ; content consultant, Finessa Ferrell.
     p. cm. -- (A bully-free world)
  ISBN 978-1-61641-848-9
  1. Bullying--Juvenile literature. 2. Bullying--Prevention--Juvenile literature. 3. Aggressiveness in children--Juvenile literature. I. Ostrom, Bob. II. Title.
  BF637.B85H3364 2013
  302.34'3--dc23
                              2011038555

TABLE OF CONTENTS

Why Do People Bully?......................................4

Class Clown 6

What to Do...8

Playground Bullies 10

What to Do...12

Online Rumors...14

What to Do...16

No-Shows 18

What to Do...20

Take the Bully Test..22

Words to Know...24

Web Sites..24

WHY DO PEOPLE
BULLY?

Bullying happens all the time. It happens at parties and at school. Cyberbullying happens on the computer and on cell phones. How can bullying be stopped? One of the most important ways is by being a good upstander. Bullies lose their power when people help those being bullied.

Bullies need to learn that every person is different and that is okay! The kids at Niceville Elementary School are learning that everyone has something great to offer. They are working together to make a bully-free world!

5

CLASS CLOWN

Carlos is making fun of Derek to hurt Derek's feelings. Carlos says he's only joking, though. Even if he says he's joking, Carlos is still a verbal bully. This means he is saying words to hurt another person on purpose. Carlos is looking for attention. He picks on Derek to make himself feel better and more powerful.

WHAT TO DO

Other kids think Carlos is being mean. What can they do? Sarah decides to act. First, she tells Carlos to knock it off. She tells him he's not being funny. Second, she supports Derek. She tells him it isn't his fault that he is being bullied. No one deserves to be bullied.

PLAYGROUND BULLIES

Joe isn't letting the smaller kids use the monkey bars on the playground. If others try, he pushes or pulls them off. This is a form of physical bullying. Kicking and hitting are physical bullying, too.

Every seven minutes a child in the United States is bullied. Kids who do those things want to make themselves look better by picking on somebody else.

WHAT TO DO

Tim wants to be an upstander. He learned the most important thing someone can do to stop bullying is to stand up for the person being bullied. First, he tells Joe to stop acting that way. He says the monkey bars belong to everyone at school. Second, he makes a joke of it. He makes Joe look silly and takes his power away.

Are you afraid he can climb higher? Come on guys! Everyone is allowed to use the monkey bars.

ONLINE RUMORS

The Internet and cell phones can be used for bullying, too. Cyberbullies can be even meaner than other types of bullies. This is because people can't always tell who they are. Text messages can send rumors fast.

Lee started a rumor about Isabel from her phone. Soon the whole class had the text message sent to them. Rumors are not okay. About 40 percent of kids have been bullied online. How can this be stopped?

WHAT TO DO

Taylor knows Lee spread this rumor and that it is not true. It is his duty to say something. Taylor should tell Lee to knock it off. Taylor should also tell an adult he trusts about what happened. This is called reporting, and it will help stop the bullying.

Next, Taylor can help Isabel deal with the rumor. Taylor can tell everyone he was at gym with Isabel and the rumor isn't true. When Lee stops getting the attention, she will stop bullying.

NO-SHOWS

Emily is being a social bully. She is pressuring others to make Ava feel and look bad. Other kinds of social bullying are teasing, gossiping, or even telling secrets sometimes. If someone wants to be hurtful on purpose and does these things, that person is a social bully. Lily wants to stop Emily's bullying. But how?

We're all invited to Ava's party, but let's all not go. It will be so funny when she realizes no one likes her.

WHAT TO DO

First, Lily should support Ava! She should talk with the other kids in class. She should let them know how mean Emily's plan is. She should get them to agree to show up at Ava's party if they say they are coming.

Second, Lily could get excited with Ava about her party. Lily can talk about how much fun it will be. She could ask Ava questions about cake and games. The other kids will get excited about the party. Everyone will probably forget about Emily's plan.

No way. I'm going to Ava's party. It's going to be so fun. You guys will miss out if you don't come.

TAKE THE
BULLY TEST

How can you tell if you ever bully? You are a bully if you do things you know will hurt people or make them feel bad. Ask yourself these questions:

- Do I feel better when I hurt other kids or take their stuff?

- Do I use my strength or size to get my way?

- Do I like to leave others out to make them feel bad?

- Have I ever spread a rumor that I knew was not true?

- Do I like teasing others?

Q Is it funny to me when I see other kids getting made fun of?

Q Have I ever kicked, punched, or hit someone?

If you answered "yes" to any of these questions, you might be a bully. Is that really how you want to be?

Of course not! Everyone makes mistakes. You can change the way you act. The first step is to say, "I'm sorry." Practice being nice to other people. Think before you say or do something. Treat others the way you want to be treated.

NOTE TO PARENTS AND CAREGIVERS

Young children often imitate their parents' or caregivers' behaviors. If you show bullying actions or use bullying language, it is likely your children will, too. They do not know their behavior is unacceptable because they see it in trusted adults. You can help prevent your student from bullying by modeling good behavior.

WORDS TO KNOW

cyberbullying—using computers and cell phones to be mean to others.

physical bullying—pushing, kicking, hitting, or touching someone in a harmful way.

reporting—telling an adult about being bullied.

rumor—talk that may not be true but is repeated by many people.

social bullying—telling secrets, spreading rumors, giving mean looks, and leaving kids out on purpose.

upstander—someone who sees bullying and stands up for the person being bullied.

verbal bullying—being mean to someone using words, such as by name-calling.

WEB SITES

To learn more about making a bully-free world, visit ABDO Group online at **www.abdopublishing.com**. Web sites about making a bully-free world are featured on our Book Links page. These links are routinely monitored and updated to provide the most current information available.